People

Communities

by Sarah L. Schuette

Consulting Editor: Gail Saunders-Smith, PhD

Capstone press.

Mankato, Minnesota

Pebble Books are published by Capstone Press,
1710 Roe Crest Drive, North Mankato, Minnesota 56003.
www.capstonepub.com

Library of Congress Cataloging-in-Publication Data
Schuette, Sarah L., 1976–
    Communities / by Sarah L. Schuette. — Rev. and updated ed.
    p. cm. — (Pebble books. People)
    Includes bibliographical references and index.
    Summary: "In simple text and photos, presents communities and the people
who live in them"— Provided by publisher.
    ISBN-13: 978-1-4296-2238-7 (hardcover)
    ISBN-10: 1-4296-2238-5 (hardcover)
    ISBN-13: 978-1-4296-3461-8 (softcover)
    ISBN-10: 1-4296-3461-8 (softcover)
    1. Communities — Juvenile literature. 2. Neighborhood — Juvenile literature.
I. Title. II. Series
HM756.S38 2009
307 — dc22
                                                   2008026949

Note to Parents and Teachers

The People set supports national social studies standards related
to individual development and identity. This book describes and
illustrates communities. The images support early readers in
understanding the text. The repetition of words and phrases helps
early readers learn new words. This book also introduces early
readers to subject-specific vocabulary words, which are defined
in the Glossary section. Early readers may need assistance to read
some words and to use the Table of Contents, Glossary, Read More,
Internet Sites, and Index sections of the book.

Table of Contents

What's a Community?

A community is a group
of people who live
in the same area.

Communities can be
big or small.
A neighborhood, town,
or city can be a community.

8

Living in a Community

Community members
take care of each other
and where they live.

Ivan waters the flowers
in his yard.

Sally picks up garbage
on the sidewalk.

Working

People have many jobs
in communities.
Kevin works
at a grocery store.

Linda works
at the police station.
She directs traffic.

Hayes is a doctor.

He gives exams.

A Nice Place

A community is
a nice place to live.

Glossary

community — a group of people who live in the same area or who have something in common with each other

direct — to show or tell someone the way to go

neighborhood — the local area around your house

town — a group of neighborhoods that forms a community

Read More

Bodden, Valerie. *A Town.* My First Look at Communities. Mankato, Minn.: Creative Education, 2008.

Gillis, Jennifer Blizin. *Neighborhood Helpers.* My Neighborhood. Vero Beach, Fla.: Rourke, 2007.

Internet Sites

FactHound offers a safe, fun way to find educator-approved Internet sites related to this book.

Here's what you do:
1. Visit *www.facthound.com*
2. Choose your grade level.
3. Begin your search.

This book's ID number is 9781429622387.

FactHound will fetch the best sites for you!

Index

Word Count: 89
Grade: 1
Early-Intervention Level: 12

Credits
Kim Brown, cover designer; Abbey Fitzgerald, book designer; Marcy Morin, photo shoot scheduler

Photo Credits
Capstone Press/Karon Dubke, all

The author dedicates this book to her friends Dan and Suzanne Buck, of Henderson, Minnesota.